Contents

1 The Finland Station

Late in the evening of 3 April 1917, a long train rumbles along the approaches to Petrograd, then the capital of Russia. In one of its lighted coaches sits Vladimir Ilyich Ulyanov, who is better known to the world as Lenin. He is returning to Russia after ten years in **exile**. He has spent those years writing **revolutionary** books, organizing his revolutionary party, the **Bolsheviks**, and waiting for the revolution which will sweep away the Russian **Tsar** and his government.

The train clanks and hisses to a halt in Petrograd's Finland Station. It is almost midnight but many are gathered to greet Lenin and the other returning exiles. There is an honour guard of revolutionary sailors on the platform, a delegation from the new Petrograd **Soviet** waiting inside the station building, a vast crowd of sympathizers waving red banners in the square beyond.

▲ A Soviet-era painting of Lenin speaking to the crowd outside Petrograd's Finland Station, shortly after his arrival on 3 April 1917.

Lenin steps from the train, briefly addresses the sailors, and walks through to the reception room once reserved for the Tsar and his family, which is now called the People's Room. The Chairman of the Petrograd Soviet steps forward to greet him, expecting a moment of shared celebration. After all, the Tsar and his government are gone.

However, Lenin almost brushes him aside. He has not come home to celebrate what has already been achieved, but to demand more – much more.

He strides through to the main square and clambers up onto the top of an armoured car that local Bolsheviks have brought along to act as a podium. He tells the hushed crowd how little the first revolution has really achieved, how little the new Provisional Government will really do for ordinary people. They need another revolution, he says, a **socialist** revolution.

At this moment few agree with him. But over the next few months he will win over the doubters in his own Bolshevik party, and go on to convince a majority of ordinary workers, soldiers and other Russians that his is the right way forward. Together they will seize power, and this second revolution will turn Russia upside-down. Lenin and his successors will do what has never been done before: they will try to create a state that provides absolutely everything for its citizens, who will therefore have no need for any private property.

They will fail. But the attempt, which begins in earnest here at the Finland Station, will be perhaps the most important political event of the 20th century. Lenin's revolution will affect everything that comes after it, both in Russia and also around the world.

Childhood and youth

Vladimir Ilyich Ulyanov, the future Lenin, was born in the Russian town of Simbirsk on 10 April 1870. His parents Ilya and Maria already had two children – Anna (born 1864) and Alexander (1866) – and they would have three more after Vladimir: Olga (1871), Dmitri (1874) and Maria (1878). As Inspector of Schools for the whole of Simbirsk province, Ilya Ulyanov held an important and respected position, and the family lived in a large house in the centre of the town.

Both Ilya and his wife were well educated, and between them they instilled in their children a love of learning. The house was full of books and the family often read to each other in the evenings.

'Volodya'

Vladimir – or 'Volodya' as the family called him – had trouble learning to walk, frequently falling over, banging his above-average-sized head and roaring with frustration. He remained a noisy boy throughout his childhood, but he also began to reveal several enduring and valuable characteristics.

◀ The Ulyanov family in 1879. Standing, left to right: Olga, Alexander and Anna. Sitting, left to right: Maria Alexandrovna (with Maria on her lap), Dmitri, Ilya Nikolayevich and Vladimir (Lenin).

People found him to be charming and likeable. He also found it hard to lie, and on one occasion when he did so – denying that he had broken a vase belonging to an aunt – his mother found him crying with guilt three months later.

▲ The house where Lenin was born in the Volga river city of Simbirsk.

He was a very clever boy, and his school record, like that of his elder brother Alexander, would turn out to be everything their father could have wished for. Both boys attended the Simbirsk Classical Gimnazia, a state school for brighter boys, from the age of nine, and both scored high marks throughout their school careers. Vladimir, in particular, was a very careful worker, always making sure he had taken everything into account. He always kept his pencils sharp.

A good report

'Extremely talented, consistently keen and accurate, Ulyanov in all classes was the top pupil and at the end of his course was awarded the gold medal as the most deserving pupil in performance, development and behaviour. Neither at the gimnazia *[school] nor outside did any occasion come to light when Ulyanov by word or deed attracted disapproving opinion from the governing authorities or teachers ...'*

(A reference written by Lenin's Headmaster Fyedor Kerensky. By a strange quirk of fate, it would be the government headed by his son Alexander Kerensky which would be overthrown by Lenin and his party in 1917)

When he was not working Vladimir loved to take part in outdoor activities, often in the company of his sister Olga. In the summer they could fish, swim or go sailing on the nearby River Volga, and in the long freezing winter there was skating, skiing and tobogganing.

In many ways it seems to have been an idyllic childhood. Vladimir was a clever, mostly healthy boy growing up in a large, prosperous and loving family. Indeed, some neighbours in Simbirsk even went so far as to call the Ulyanovs 'the beautiful family'. The children's futures seemed assured.

Russia

In the late 19th century, the Russian Empire included European Russia, much of Poland, the vast Asian region known as Siberia, and present-day Finland, Lithuania, Latvia, Estonia, Moldova, Belarus, Ukraine, Georgia, Azerbaijan, Armenia, Turkmenistan, Kazakhstan, Uzbekistan, Kirghizstan and Tadjikistan. Finland and Poland became independent states in 1917 and 1918. The rest remained part of the Union of Soviet Socialist Republics (or Soviet Union) until its break-up in the early 1990s.

Tragedies

But then, out of this clear blue sky, tragedy struck not once but twice. In 1886, when Vladimir was fifteen, Ilya Ulyanov died quite suddenly, probably from a brain haemorrhage. By this time Alexander was already at university in the Russian capital **St Petersburg**, and during the period of shock and grief Vladimir had to act as the man of the family. He found it difficult, and for a while his behaviour was much worse than usual, but life went on. The family made efforts to economize, and Vladimir continued with his studies, expecting soon to follow his brother to university.

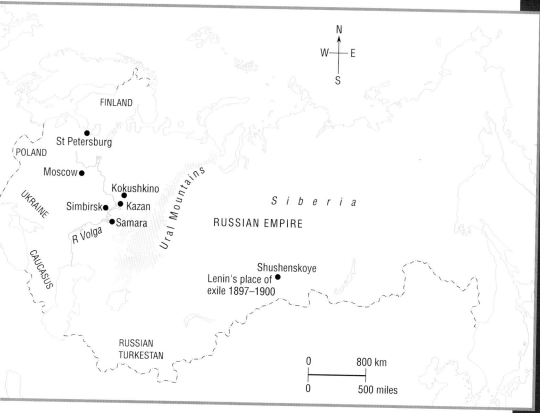

▲ *Map of the Russian Empire, c.1890.*

Ilya and Maria had always been 'progressive' – they wanted Russia to modernize itself, to become more like the **democracies** of Western Europe – but they expected change to come gradually, and to be brought about by reason and persuasion. Their eldest son Alexander, having moved from the sleepy town of Simbirsk to Russia's capital, had become terribly aware of how bad things really were for most of his fellow Russians. A few thousand families had most of the money and held most of the power, and millions of **peasants** lived as virtual slaves, many in terrible poverty. Famines were common. There was no parliament, only an hereditary Emperor or '**Tsar**' who ruled as he saw fit. There was no legal way of opposing this state of affairs.

There were groups of men and women who felt strongly enough about the situation to form illegal opposition groups, and by 1886 Alexander felt motivated to join one of them. This group's intention was to assassinate the Tsar in order to force a change, but the police caught them before they had time to carry out their plan. At the trial, Alexander bravely took most of the blame on himself, and he was sentenced to death. On 8 May 1887 he was hanged in St Petersburg.

▲ *Vladimir's brother, Alexander Ulyanov.*

A brother's legacy

The effect on the family was devastating. Maria Ulyanova, who had still not recovered from losing her husband, was driven to thoughts of suicide. Former friends and colleagues shunned the family as a whole – no one wanted to be associated with the relatives of a convicted **terrorist**.

Vladimir tried to comfort his mother. He sympathized with his sister Olga, who was being cold-shouldered by classmates at school, and he played games with his younger brother and sister to take their minds off the tragedy. Vladimir kept his own feelings mostly to himself, but he must have felt angry as well as sad. He seems to have had no doubt that Alexander had acted with the best of motives. 'It must mean that he had to act like this,' he told a friend. 'He couldn't act in any other way.'

3 In his brother's footsteps

Despite everything, Vladimir managed to pass his final school exams with maximum scores in all ten subjects. Such marks would have ensured a place in **St Petersburg** University for most young men, but not the brother of a convicted **terrorist**. Vladimir was forced to settle for studying law at his father's old university at Kazan, some 140 kilometres (87 miles) north of Simbirsk. The whole family decided between them that they would move with him.

In that summer of 1887, as he waited to start at university, Vladimir read a great deal. One book that had belonged to Alexander appealed to him

▲ *Lenin in 1887, the year his brother was executed.*

enormously. The heroes of Nikolai Chernyshevski's novel *What is to be Done?* were a group of **socialist** activists, who were caught up in the struggle for change in the **Tsar**'s Russia. Their calls for **democracy**, for **women's rights**, and for an end to the oppression (harsh rule and treatment) of minorities, all made sense to Vladimir. He may have imagined his brother, or perhaps even himself in the future, as Chernyshevski's upright hero, putting wrongs to right.

Kazan

At Kazan University Vladimir soon got involved in student politics, and after only three months he was expelled.

He was to leave both the university and the city for taking part in demonstrations against the authorities. The family moved temporarily to Kokushkino, an estate in the country owned by his mother Maria Ulyanova's family. There Vladimir continued what he now considered his real education, reading the works of important European thinkers. He was particularly interested in the theories and political conclusions of Karl Marx. When the family was allowed to return to Kazan in September 1888, Vladimir quickly resumed contacts with his politically involved friends.

He wanted to resume his studies, either at Kazan University or abroad, but his requests were refused, and his mother decided that they would be better off living somewhere else. A friend of Vladimir's elder sister Anna arranged the purchase of a small estate further down the Volga River in the Samara region, and the family moved there in May 1889. His mother encouraged Vladimir to take a hand in managing the estate, but he was much more interested in continuing with his reading.

The reluctant lawyer

Eventually the persistent requests paid off, and in 1890 Vladimir was allowed to resume his studies as an **external student** at St Petersburg University. Brilliant as ever, he managed to complete the four-year course in less than one, and to pass the examinations with ease. In the meantime, however, tragedy had again struck the family. After only a short illness his favourite sister Olga died in St Petersburg on 8 May 1891, the fourth anniversary of Alexander's execution. Vladimir returned to Samara and began practising as a lawyer. He also resumed his political activity.

Karl Marx

Karl Marx was a 19th-century German **philosopher** who believed he had worked out how society changes. He thought that throughout history each ruling class – each group of people who dominated a society through either force or wealth or a combination of the two – inevitably created their own opposition. In his time the **bourgeoisie** – the owners of land, industry and communications and banks – was the ruling class in the most advanced countries, but to make their world work its members needed a growing army of ordinary workers.

Marx believed that these workers would eventually get so numerous and so fed up with making wealth for other people that they would kick out the bourgeoisie and rule in their place. Because they would then be a big majority of the population, their rule would be fairer for most people. It would be called **socialism**.

Marx had many facts to back up his theory, and many people came to believe that he was right in his predictions. They were called **Marxists** or Marxist socialists.

▶ *Karl Marx, the economist, philosopher and founder of modern* **communism.** *Lenin applied the ideas of Marx to Russian conditions.*

There seems to have been no doubt that Vladimir was more interested in politics than law. He was now every bit as committed to the overthrow of the Tsar and the rest of the Russian ruling class as his brother Alexander had been. The difference lay in the brothers' temperaments and the methods that they preferred. Alexander had been too emotional, too quick to sacrifice himself. Vladimir would not make the same mistake. The theories of Marx told him that time was on his side because there were wider forces working to undermine the old order, and that the most important thing was to understand and harness those forces. Individual acts, no matter how brave or romantic, would achieve little or nothing.

In the summer of 1892 a huge famine raged through the Volga region, but Vladimir, almost alone among his friends, refused to support relief efforts. The famine, he said, was an inevitable consequence of the way the country was run, and by supporting the relief efforts people were, in effect, supporting the Tsar. Only a **revolution**, he believed, could bring an end to famines.

▼ *The Volga River at Kazan, where Lenin attended university in the autumn of 1887.*

4 The young revolutionary

By the summer of 1893 Vladimir Ulyanov was tired of Samara, tired of life in the provinces. He left the family home and moved to **St Petersburg**, where he registered as assistant to another lawyer. However, he did no legal work, relying on a monthly allowance from his mother for his living expenses. His real work was politics, a daily round of reading, writing, talking and organizing.

He had now read almost everything Marx had written, and felt able to use Marx's ideas in his own writing. His knowledge and cleverness shone through at meetings, as did his competitive attitude. Fellow political thinkers were not only out-argued, but also made to question their own level of commitment. Vladimir Ulyanov was not prepared to give anyone an easy ride.

He was now 24 years of age, but the loss of most of his hair made him look older. There was nothing 'bohemian' (unconventional) about him: he hated untidiness and waste, was careful with money, kept his beard trim and his shoes well repaired. The only thing Ulyanov was careless about was his own health, which was unfortunate. Most of his family seem to have suffered from stomach problems at one time or another, and his irregular eating habits took a heavy toll. He suffered badly from headaches and had trouble sleeping.

He does not seem to have been very interested in romance, but it was during this period that he met his future wife, Nadezhda Krupskaya. It is hard to know for certain, but their relationship seems to have been based more on political friendship than on strong passion.

The future Mrs Lenin

Nadezhda Krupskaya was born into a reasonably well-to-do family in 1869. Her father had been an officer in the **Tsar**'s army before his daughter was born, but had been dismissed for being too lenient with Polish protestors, and thereafter had a succession of different jobs. Her mother wrote children's books. Nadezhda was well educated and, like her future husband, slowly became convinced of the correctness of Marx's **revolutionary** teachings. She first met Vladimir Ulyanov at a Marxist discussion group in 1894.

▶ *Lenin's wife Nadezhda Krupskaya, photographed around the time the two met in St Petersburg.*

A revolutionary network

In March 1895, the authorities finally gave Ulyanov permission to travel abroad. The trip lasted for several months. He took the opportunity to get medical advice on his stomach troubles, but his main aim was to visit the leaders of Russian **Marxism**, all of whom were living in West European **exile**. In Geneva he met the most important of these, Georgi Plekhanov, and the two men got on well. Plekhanov was pleased to hear that he had so many followers back in Russia, and they discussed Ulyanov's scheme for launching a newspaper. After meeting several other prominent Marxists, Ulyanov returned to St Petersburg full of optimism.

With the help of a new ally, Yuli Martov, Ulyanov shifted the emphasis of their political activity in St Petersburg from discussion groups about theories to agitation among the workers. He wrote a leaflet for striking textile workers explaining their legal rights. At last he had done something to really worry the authorities, and on 9 December he was duly arrested.

▲ Lenin and Yuli Martov (fourth and sixth from left) with a group of fellow Marxists in St Petersburg, 1895.

Ulyanov spent the next fourteen months in the St Petersburg prison awaiting sentence and working on his future book *The Development of Capitalism in Russia.* His family sent in food and pencils, and he smuggled out invisible messages written in milk – heating turned the writing brown.

Dancing feet

'Vladimir Ilyich said that in the preliminary prison he always polished the cell floor himself since this was a good form of gymnastics. And so he acted like a real old floor-polisher – with his hands held behind him, he would begin to dance to and fro across the cell with a brush or a rag under his foot.'

(Dmitri Ulyanov, remembering a conversation with his older brother)

Siberia

In January 1897, Ulyanov was finally sentenced to three years' exile in Siberia, but even this proved easier than he might have expected. He was sent to Shushenskoye in 'Siberian Italy', so-called because of its mild climate. Nadezhda Krupskaya, also sentenced, was allowed to join him on condition that they were married. Ulyanov worked hard on his book and enjoyed himself in the Siberian wilderness, hunting, fishing and gathering wild mushrooms. His wife thought his skating style was rather extravagant, and accused him of 'strutting like a chicken'.

▲ The cottage in Shushenskoye, Siberia, where Vladimir Ulyanov and his wife Nadezhda Krupskaya spent their years of internal exile.

In the summer of 1898 he finished *The Development of Capitalism in Russia*. His main argument, supported by a wealth of statistics, was that Russia was becoming a **capitalist** country just like those in western Europe. This implied that Russia should also have a middle-class **democracy**, and that this would lead to a **socialist** revolution. As the century drew to an end, Vladimir Ulyanov was laying the theoretical groundwork for his future actions.

5 A party to lead

When his term of Siberian **exile**
came to an end in 1900, Ulyanov
was also granted permission to
leave Russia. He travelled back to
St Petersburg full of ideas and
enthusiasm for the struggle
ahead, but also worried by what
he had heard of all the arguments
among the Russian **Marxist**
exiles. On arrival, he found that
there was indeed little or no
agreement on what should be
done next. The Russian Social-
Democratic Labour Party had
finally been formed in 1898,
principally under Georgi
Plekhanov's direction, but there
was little agreement as to what
the party should do. Some
members wanted to leave
everything to **trade unions**, others wanted to launch a new
terrorist campaign. Some seemed quite happy to wait until
the middle classes had overthrown the **Tsar** and created a
democracy before they began seriously working for
socialism.

▲ *Vladimir Ulyanov in 1900, soon after
his release from Siberian exile.*

Iskra

Ulyanov's first priority was to press for the creation of a
newspaper. This, he thought, would both provide a link
between the exiles and their fellow Marxists inside Russia
and help to create a unified policy or 'party line'. Plekhanov
agreed with him, and the first edition of *Iskra* (which means
'The Spark') was printed in the last few days of 1900.

◀ *Georgi Plekhanov, the father of Russian Marxism. A founding member of the Russian Social-Democratic Labour Party and an editor of* Iskra, *he fell out with Lenin in 1903.*

Ulyanov was only one of six editors – all of whom also wrote – but he was the most active and the most determined.

The first *Iskra* editorial was a clear message to all those Marxists who were happy to wait for either the middle class or the working class to spontaneously produce a revolution in Russia. The whole point of a socialist party, he wrote, was to urge the masses on, to point out where their real interests lay when they did not realize it for themselves. The party's job was to lead, not follow.

The need for organization

'If we have a strongly organized party, a single strike may grow into a political demonstration, into a political victory over the regime. If we have a strongly organized party, a rebellion in a single locality may spread into a victorious revolution.'

(Vladimir Ulyanov, writing in the first edition of *Iskra*, December 1900)

What is to be Done?

With the paper up and running, Ulyanov wrote an enormously influential pamphlet explaining his ideas. He gave it the same title – *What is to be Done?* – as the novel by Chernyshevski which had so influenced him and his older brother, but it had a very different theme. Ulyanov was writing a practical pamphlet – almost a manual – on how to create a revolution in Russia. He signed it with a new pseudonym (false name), the one by which he would now be known: Lenin.

According to *What is to be Done?*, the only real option was to create a party which operated in secret, which was disciplined, united and highly centralized. The party's job was to convince the working class that its arguments were right. The working class would then overthrow the Tsarist government and ease the sufferings of the mass of the Russian people.

This made a great deal of sense. There was clearly no hope of organizing support in full view of the government – the organizers would simply be arrested. It was also clear that a party operating 'underground' would need both direction from a single-minded central leadership and strong discipline.

However, there was a lot of opposition to Lenin's views. Some thought his apparent fondness for direct action verged on support of terrorism, while some were simply jealous of his growing importance in the party. More importantly, some pointed out how **undemocratic** his plans were: party policy would be decided by only a very few people.

Home life

Lenin and Krupskaya were living in Munich during this period. He wrote, she acted as his secretary, and her mother, who also lived with them, did the cooking.

Lenin needed absolute silence to work in, and even used to walk around his study on tiptoe to avoid disturbing his own train of thought. For exercise he went on long cycle rides, and took great care of his bicycle, treating it like 'a surgical instrument'.

The couple had not had any children, which was a source of great sadness to them both. In their leisure hours they read novels, and frequently attended the theatre and concerts. Lenin, like most of the Ulyanovs, was passionately fond of music by the composer Richard Wagner, and sometimes he would get so excited by the music that he had to leave the concert hall. All through his life Lenin would strive, and usually succeed, in repressing his own passionate nature. He was determined to be guided by his mind and not by his feelings.

In 1902 Lenin and Krupskaya moved to London, where *Iskra* was now to be produced. Lenin loved the libraries and parks and hated the English food. He and Krupskaya often took long rides around the city on open-topped double-decker buses. One morning, a young **revolutionary** called Leon Trotsky came to the house to introduce himself. He and Lenin quickly became friends.

The Second Congress

The long-awaited Second Congress of the Russian Social-Democratic Labour Party took place, first in Brussels and then in London, over several weeks in 1903. The differences of opinion inside the party had been buried for a while, but they had not gone away, and the Congress proved a bad-tempered and divisive affair. On one important vote Lenin and his supporters won by a majority, emphasizing this by calling themselves the **Bolsheviks**, or 'those in the majority'.

But most of the time he found himself outvoted, and it became clear that he had few supporters among the party's members in Russia. More supported the **Mensheviks** ('those in a minority'). In the arguments which followed, he ended up resigning from the committee that ran *Iskra*.

By the beginning of 1904, Lenin was at a low point. His stomach problems, headaches and sleeping problems had returned, and many Bolsheviks were now refusing to support him. That summer, he and Krupskaya took a long walking holiday in the Alps to get away from it all. When they returned, Lenin felt ready to reorganize those supporters he still had, to convene a new Party Congress, and to start a new newspaper to rival *Iskra*. The Bolsheviks, he was convinced, would yet win the party's **civil war**.

▲ Delegates to the Second Congress of the Russian Social-Democratic Labour Party in 1903. Lenin is second from the left in the top row; his wife Nadezhda Krupskaya, far left in the bottom row.

6 Waiting in the wings

On Sunday 9 January 1905, a peaceful procession approached the **Tsar**'s Winter Palace in St Petersburg, armed only with a petition for **civil rights** and greater **democracy**. The Tsar's soldiers opened fire, and over 70 marchers were killed. This 'Bloody Sunday' ushered in more than a year of disturbances throughout the Russian Empire. Strikes and demonstrations became an almost daily affair, and the Tsar's authority was further weakened by a series of catastrophic defeats in the Russo-Japanese War. New councils or '**soviets**' sprang up everywhere. Refused democracy by the Tsar, the people were electing their own alternative governments all across the Russian Empire.

▼ *A painting showing the Tsar's troops attacking the peaceful demonstration on 'Bloody Sunday', 9 January 1905.*

Watching from a distance

The **Marxist exiles** in western Europe were overjoyed by the **revolutionary** activity in their native land, but argued amongst themselves about how they should react. In April 1905, a Party Congress was called with the intention of unifying the divided party, but most of Lenin's opponents refused to attend, and he was able to reassert his authority over his **Bolshevik** colleagues. As usual, he favoured direct action. An **armed insurrection** was needed, he told the Congress. A revolutionary government should be set up, the property of the rich confiscated (taken), and mass terror unleashed. Lenin sounded like a real revolutionary and his words electrified his audience.

Call to action

'Go to the youth. Organize at once and everywhere fighting brigades among students, and particularly among workers. Let them arm themselves immediately with whatever weapons they can obtain – a knife, a revolver, a kerosene-soaked rag for setting fires ... Let the squads begin to train for immediate operations. Some can undertake to assassinate a spy or blow up a police station, others can attack a bank to expropriate funds for an insurrection. Let every squad learn, if only by beating up police.'

(Lenin, speaking from abroad in 1905)

As the year unfolded, however, Lenin made no move to return to Russia. Many of his fellow Marxists did so – Trotsky, for example, soon became a leading member of the **St Petersburg Soviet** – but Lenin did not see how his own arrest would help the revolution. It was only when the Tsar issued his October Manifesto, promising civil rights for the Russian people and pardoning all political exiles, that he felt able to set foot once more in his homeland.

Back in Russia

Before leaving for Russia, Lenin wrote to the Bolsheviks'
Combat Committee, and bitterly complained that 'there has
been talk about bombs *for more than a year* and yet not a
single bomb has been made!' By early November, however,
when he arrived back in St Petersburg, the revolutionary
upsurge had clearly passed its peak. Lenin set himself to
understanding exactly what had happened, attending meeting
after meeting and talking to as many people as he could.

Meanwhile, the Tsar's regime was slowly regaining its strength
and confidence, and in the summer of 1906 Lenin and other
Bolshevik leaders thought it wise to leave St Petersburg. They
moved to Finland, then a fairly detached portion of the
Russian Empire, and for a year or so tried to run the party
from there. Eventually even that haven proved unsafe.

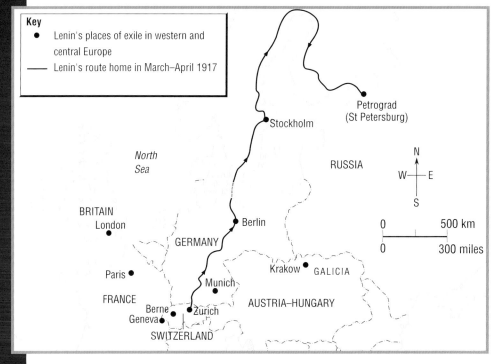

Key
● Lenin's places of exile in western and central Europe
— Lenin's route home in March–April 1917

Petrograd (St Petersburg)

Stockholm

North Sea

RUSSIA

BRITAIN
London

Berlin

GERMANY

Krakow ● GALICIA

Paris ●

Munich

FRANCE

AUSTRIA–HUNGARY

Berne Zurich
Geneva

SWITZERLAND

0   500 km
0   300 miles

▲ *Map showing Lenin's places of exile, 1901–17.*

Warned that a police raid was imminent, Lenin decided to catch a ferry to Sweden from an island off the Finnish coast. To reach the island he had to walk across a half-frozen bay, and the two local guides who escorted him were both too drunk to offer much help. On one occasion the ice broke beneath him and Lenin only just managed to scramble to safety. 'What a stupid way to die!' he apparently said.

Exile once more

Despite Lenin's objections, the Bolshevik headquarters was moved to Paris in 1908 and for the next four years he and Krupskaya shared a house there with her mother and his youngest sister Maria. Maria, like Lenin's older sister Anna and brother Dmitri, was active in the revolutionary movement.

In Paris Lenin read, wrote and schemed. Each day he rode his bicycle to the famous library, the Bibliothèque Nationale, and on one occasion he was knocked off his bike by a car. He used his legal training to sue the motorist, who, much to Lenin's glee, turned out to be a nobleman.

Lenin's 'Hm'

'He enjoyed fun, and when he laughed his whole body shook, really bursting with laughter, sometimes until tears came into his eyes. There was an endless scale of shade and meaning in his inarticulate "hm" – ranging from bitter sarcasm to cautious doubt, and there was often in it the keen humour given only to one who sees far ahead and knows well the satanic absurdities [the terrible ridiculousness] of life.'

(Russian writer Maxim Gorky, who first met Lenin in 1908)

◀ Lenin playing chess with a fellow Russian Marxist, A. A. Bogdanov. Both men were staying with the Russian writer Maxim Gorky on the Italian island of Capri, May 1908.

It was during this period that he began a love affair with another revolutionary, Inessa Armand. It seems certain that she was in love with him, and probable that he was also in love with her. But when, after two years or so of the affair, Lenin was forced to choose between Armand and his wife, he chose Krupskaya. His wife was his co-worker and nothing, not even love, was more important than his work.

War

In 1912, Lenin and Krupskaya moved to the Polish city of Krakow, in what was then the Austro-Hungarian province of Galicia. They had been there for two years when World War I suddenly broke out. As Russian nationals in Austria–Hungary they qualified as enemy aliens, and Lenin spent several days in jail while his friends tried to convince the Austrian authorities that Lenin liked the Tsar even less than they did. Eventually he and Krupskaya were allowed to travel to Switzerland, which was neutral (did not support either side in the war).

Once safe, Lenin was able to take in what had happened elsewhere in Europe. The German Social Democrats, supposedly Marxists like himself, had supported the German Kaiser (emperor) and his war! They were not the only ones. **Socialists** all over Europe were acting as if a person's nationality was more important than a person's class. Lenin was outraged – the European working class was being betrayed by its socialist leaders, by people who should have known better.

His counterblast was to call for a European **civil war**. Each national working class, he said, should work for the defeat of its own government. He particularly longed for a Russian defeat, because that, he thought, would probably mean the end of the Tsar.

For the moment, few supported him. Deprived of contact with Russia and ignored by many of his fellow exiles, he felt increasingly isolated. The death of his mother, whom he dearly loved, was another blow.

As always he hid from his feelings by working. In 1916, he wrote his pamphlet *Imperialism: A Higher Stage of Capitalism*, which was destined to be one of the most influential works of the 20th century. The whole world economy was now linked together, he explained, which meant that **capitalism** was now vulnerable everywhere. Not just, as Marx had said, in the rich, developed countries like Britain, Germany and USA, but in the poorer, less developed ones like Russia as well.

When would the first cracks appear? In January 1917, a pessimistic Lenin told a meeting that 'we, the old people, perhaps won't survive until the decisive battles of the forthcoming revolution'.

7 Two revolutions

In February 1917, the Tsarist regime finally began to disintegrate under the strains of World War I. Demonstrations multiplied, strikes erupted, and the **soviets** sprang back to life. The **Tsar**, realizing that he could no longer rely on his soldiers, was forced to abdicate. A new, provisional (temporary) government was set up, but it did not withdraw Russia from the war.

In March, news of the Tsar's fall reached the **exiles** in Switzerland, but Lenin allowed himself only a day's celebration. This was the beginning, not the end. He sent off messages to the **Bolsheviks** in Petrograd (as **St Petersburg** was now called) demanding that there be no cooperation with the **Mensheviks** and no support for the war. In an open letter to the Russian people he told them: 'You performed miracles of proletarian [working class] heroism yesterday in overthrowing the Tsarist **monarchy** ... You will again have to perform miracles of heroism to overthrow the rule of the landlords and capitalists'.

The April Theses

Lenin had to get back to Russia. The Germans, thinking that the arrival in Petrograd of anti-war campaigners could only benefit them, agreed to let the exiles through. In late March, Lenin, Krupskaya and 30 others set off on a week-long journey by train and boat through Germany, Sweden and Finland. They finally arrived at Petrograd's Finland Station on 3 April.

FOR DETAILS ON KEY PEOPLE OF LENIN'S TIME, SEE PAGES 58–9.

En route, Lenin had read in a Petrograd paper that Kamenev and Stalin – two of the other Bolshevik leaders – had been offering support to the provisional government. He was furious, and on arrival he wasted no time in making his own position clear. The time had come, he told the crowd outside the Finland Station, to destroy capitalism throughout Europe.

The next day he presented a set of plans to the Bolshevik Central Committee (ruling group): his 'April Theses'. In these he claimed that the Provisional Government, as a **bourgeois** or middle-class government, could neither end the war nor satisfy the other needs of the huge majority of the Russian people. A second, **socialist** revolution was needed. However, the April Theses ignored what had previously been accepted by most Marxists — that capitalism had to be fully developed in a country before socialism was possible — and they were rejected by thirteen votes to two. One leading Bolshevik called them 'the delusions of a lunatic'.

Winning the argument

This was frustrating, but Lenin did not change his mind. He believed time was on his side, and he was right. The provisional government was unable to solve the worsening problems of war and the economy, and sooner or later it was going to be destroyed by them. Then, the choice, as Lenin saw it, would be between going back and going forward. By the end of April he had convinced most of the other Bolshevik leaders that he was right.

▼ *Lenin addressing a political meeting in Moscow. The man standing beside the podium is Leon Trotsky.*

What Russia needed, he said, was an end to the war, nationalization of industry and the banks (having them run by the government rather than privately), land for the **peasants**, workers' control of the factories, and fairer treatment for the various minority peoples. It needed a Bolshevik government.

The speaker

'He was neither a great orator nor a first-rate lecturer ... He was never boring, on account of his mimic's liveliness and the reasoned conviction which drove him. His customary gestures consisted of raising his hand to underline the importance of what he had said, and then bending towards the audience, smiling and earnest, his palms spread out in an act of demonstration: "It is obvious, isn't it?"'

(Victor Serge, in his *Memoirs of a Revolutionary*)

Leader in waiting

Lenin had started to dress more smartly, having been persuaded to buy a new suit and shoes in Sweden. His trademark floppy worker's cap contrasted with the more formal headgear worn by most political leaders. Unlike most of the latter he was obviously enjoying the revolution. In fact, he was in his element.

He was also eating badly and exhausting himself. In late June, he decided to take a short break in the country, and as luck would have it this coincided with a major crisis in Petrograd. The provisional government's latest offensive against the Germans was failing badly, and for a few days in mid-July it looked as though popular pressure might bring it down. The Bolsheviks, including the hastily returned Lenin, hesitated.

The provisional government took heart, turned on the Bolsheviks, and tried to arrest the party's leaders. Lenin was forced into hiding in a friend's house, and eventually escaped to Finland.

Lenin waited and fretted in Finland, wondering if he had missed his chance. During August, he worked on *State and Revolution*, a pamphlet outlining his hopes for the future. A socialist **revolution** would create a **dictatorship** of the workers and peasants, he wrote, but once all traces of the capitalist past had been removed this government would become more **democratic**, and eventually under **communism** the need for a state would disappear altogether.

▲ *The attic in a barn at Razliv near Petrograd, where Lenin lived and worked when he went into hiding in the summer of 1917.*

Seizure of power

The situation in Petrograd continued to deteriorate. The provisional government seemed to be falling apart; the Bolsheviks now held majorities in the crucial Petrograd and Moscow soviets. The time for an armed uprising had arrived, Lenin wrote to the other Bolshevik leaders on 12 September.

They disagreed, and Lenin decided he had to return to Petrograd to persuade them. He finally arrived at the end of the month, disguised as a minister of the Lutheran church (a branch of the Protestant church). He had shaved off his beard and wore a wig, which he had difficulty keeping on his head.

▶ Lenin without his beard, during his months on the run from the provisional government in the summer of 1917.

The leader

'A short, stocky figure, with a big head set down on his shoulders, bald and bulging. Little eyes, a snubbish nose, wide generous mouth, and heavy chin; clean-shaven now but already beginning to bristle with the well-known beard of his past and future. Dressed in shabby clothes, his trousers much too long for him. Unimpressive, to be the idol of a mob, loved and revered as perhaps few leaders in history have been.'

(Lenin at a meeting in October 1917, as described by American writer John Reed in *Ten Days That Shook The World*, his famous account of the revolution)

The crucial meeting of the Bolshevik Central Committee took place on 10 October. Lenin – angry, impatient and impassioned – spoke for over an hour, and the debate that followed lasted until dawn. An **armed insurrection** was decided on by ten votes to two.

Two weeks later, on the night of 24–25 October, it began. Leon Trotsky did most of the organizing, as groups of armed party members, many of them soldiers and sailors, seized key locations in Petrograd: the post and telegraph offices, the rail terminals, the state bank, the **Tsar**'s Winter Palace. By the evening of the 25th the city was in the hands of the Bolsheviks. 'Lenin's wide awake eyes rested on my tired face,' Trotsky wrote later. '"You know," he said hesitantly, "to pass suddenly from persecution and underground living to a position of power... It makes one dizzy." We looked at one another and smiled.'

▲ *A motorized unit of Red Guards in Petrograd during the October Revolution.*

8 The first year

Although their control was far from complete, the **Bolsheviks** now set out to form a government for all Russia. They called it the Council of People's **Commissars**, which was abbreviated as **Sovnarkom**. The All-Russian Congress of Soviets approved Lenin's appointment as Chairman of Sovnarkom, and the appointment of other Bolshevik leaders to other government jobs. Trotsky, for example, became the Commissar for Foreign Affairs and Stalin was appointed Commissar for Nationalities.

Promises ...

During its first winter in power Sovnarkom introduced a series of astonishingly far-reaching decrees or laws. First, as promised, Lenin announced that Russia was withdrawing from World War I. On the Eastern front, hostilities ceased, and many of the Russian troops simply took off in the direction of home. Second, the Decree on Land not only confiscated all land owned by the nobility and the Church, but effectively handed all land not already owned by the **peasants** over to them.

Free schooling was promised for all, and women were now to be considered the equals of men. All titles except 'Citizen' and 'Comrade' were abolished; there would be no more princes or dukes. The maximum length of the working day was reduced to eight hours. The minority nations of the Russian Empire, like the Ukrainians and the Georgians, were to be given more control over their own affairs. These measures, and not the mere fact of seizing power, constituted the real **revolution**.

... And threats

Many people, worn down by the chaos of war and tired of corrupt and incompetent rulers, welcomed these changes. But there was another side to the coin.

If the changes were to last, then the Bolsheviks had to stay in power, and making sure of that meant taking measures which were much less popular. Newspapers were shut down for 'inciting resistance to Sovnarkom'. Previously planned elections to a new Constituent Assembly were allowed to go ahead, but the assembly itself was closed down by force because the Bolsheviks won only a quarter of the seats. More significantly for the future, on December 1917 Lenin sanctioned the creation of the Extraordinary Commission for Combating Counter-revolution and Sabotage or **Cheka**. The function of this armed **political police** force was to defend the revolution against its growing number of enemies.

The need for terror

'The workers and soldiers of Petrograd must realize that no one will help them except themselves. Malpractices [wrongdoings] are blatant, profiteering [making excessive profits] is monstrous, but what have the masses of soldiers and peasants done to combat this? Unless the masses are roused to spontaneous action, we won't get anywhere ... Until we apply terror to speculators – shooting on the spot – we won't get anywhere. Looters should likewise be dealt with resolutely – by shooting on the spot.'

(Lenin, speaking to the leaders of the Petrograd Soviet in January 1918)

Enemies everywhere

The most immediate threat to the Bolsheviks' survival in the winter of 1917–18 was the German army. The Russians had stopped fighting but the Germans were threatening to keep marching eastward if the Bolsheviks did not sign a peace treaty that handed over huge areas of the old empire to Germany. Most of the Bolshevik leaders thought it would be a betrayal of the German working class to sign a deal with their government.

They preferred to let the Germans come, and then influence them from within. Lenin thought this was unrealistic – he wanted to sign, because otherwise he feared the whole revolution would be swept aside. The argument went on for weeks, until Lenin's threat of resignation finally won him a majority of votes. The Treaty of Brest-Litovsk, ending the war with Germany, was signed on 3 March 1918.

▲ Lenin reading Pravda at his desk in the **Kremlin**, 16 October 1918.

There was no shortage of other enemies for the Bolsheviks to face. The other **revolutionary** groups – the **Mensheviks**, the Socialist Revolutionaries (the party which represented most peasants) and the anarchists (who wanted to abolish all government) – all complained and plotted, but for the moment these were the least of Lenin's worries.

Many peasants, dissatisfied with the price they were being paid for grain, refused to sell it at all, and the shortages of food in the cities grew more serious. The upper classes, who had lost property and power in the revolution, had not given up hope of turning back the clock, and '**White**' **armies** led by officers of the old Imperial Army were springing into existence in several areas. The **Tsar**'s **allies** in World War I, who felt both betrayed by the Bolsheviks' separate peace and alarmed at the threat of a spreading revolution, were sending troops to help the Whites.

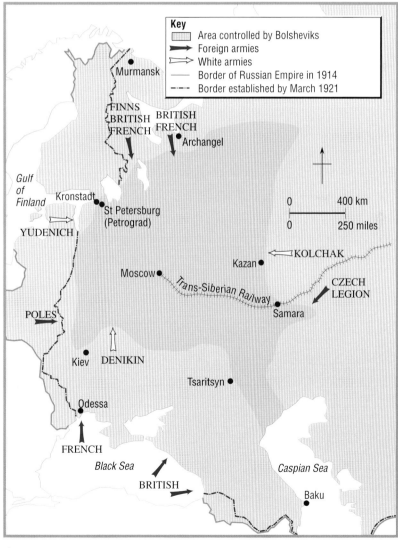

Key
- Area controlled by Bolsheviks
- Foreign armies
- White armies
- Border of Russian Empire in 1914
- Border established by March 1921

Murmansk

FINNS
BRITISH
FRENCH

BRITISH
FRENCH
Archangel

Gulf of Finland

Kronstadt

St Petersburg (Petrograd)

YUDENICH

0   400 km
0   250 miles

Kazan

KOLCHAK

Moscow

Trans-Siberian Railway

CZECH LEGION

POLES

Samara

Kiev   DENIKIN

Tsaritsyn

Odessa

FRENCH

Black Sea

BRITISH

Caspian Sea

Baku

▲ *Map showing Russia during the civil war, 1918–20.*

▲ *An armoured train of the Tenth Red Army about to leave for the front from the town of Tsaritsyn during the first year of the civil war.*

At the helm

While the new **Red Army** of revolutionary fighters, under Trotsky's direction, sought to counter these threats, Lenin worked away in the new Russian capital of Moscow. He and Krupskaya had a flat in the **Kremlin**, but she too had a full-time job – as a Deputy-Commissar for Education – and they did not see that much of each other.

Lenin was not safe even in Moscow – on one occasion his car was fired on by trigger-happy guards, on another criminals held him up at gunpoint. In August 1918 he was shot and seriously wounded by Fanya Kaplan, a Socialist Revolutionary. The Cheka's response was savage: Kaplan and hundreds of others were shot.

By this time the regime was clearly fighting for its life, and terror was one way of fighting back. If Lenin had any regrets about how bloodstained his regime was becoming, he kept them to himself.

An enemy's impression

'He looked at the first glance more like a provincial grocer than a leader of men. Yet in those steely eyes there was something that arrested my attention, something in that quizzing, half-contemptuous, half-smiling look which spoke of boundless self-confidence and conscious superiority.'

(British diplomat R.H. Bruce Lockhart, who talked to Lenin early in 1918 about possible cooperation between their two governments)

Most likely he had none: he simply told himself that the revolution's survival was more important than middle-class morality. When the news of the Tsar's execution in captivity reached him in a meeting, he simply passed on the message to those around the table and then continued with what he had been saying.

▲ *Lenin speaking in Red Square on the first anniversary of the October Revolution, 26 October 1918.*

Key dates: 1917–18

1917	• February	First Russian Revolution
	• April	Lenin returns to Russia; produces April Theses
	• July	Lenin forced into hiding
	• October	Second Russian Revolution brings Bolsheviks to power
	• December	Formation of Cheka
1918	• March	The Treaty of Brest-Litovsk ends war with Germany
	• July	Execution of Tsar and family

9 Fighting for survival

In November 1918, World War I ended in a German defeat. Lenin cancelled the Treaty of Brest-Litovsk, forcing the Germans out of those areas they had occupied. But there were still many foreign troops on Russian soil, including British in Archangel, French in the Crimea, American and Japanese in eastern Siberia. The **Bolsheviks**, who in March 1918 had renamed themselves the **Communist** Party, fought back by forming the Communist International, or **Comintern**, to fight against capitalist governments everywhere. Marxists from all over the world were invited to attend the first Congress in March 1919.

▲ Lenin (second from right) chairing a meeting at the first Congress of Comintern in the Kremlin, Moscow, March 1919.

Welcome to the Revolution

'"Have you brought your families with you? I could put them up in palaces, which I know is very nice on some occasions, but it is impossible to heat them. You'd better go to Moscow. Here, we are besieged people in a besieged city. Hunger-riots may start, the Finns may swoop on us, the British may attack. Typhus has killed so many people that we can't manage to bury them; luckily they are frozen. If work is what you want, there's plenty of it!" And she told passionately of the Soviet achievement: school-building, children's centres, relief for pensioners, free medical assistance, the theatres open to all ...'

(Victor Serge, recounting his group's welcome to Petrograd by Bolshevik leader Lilina Zinoviev in January 1919)

Some of the foreign troops were withdrawn in the first half of 1919 but by this time the homegrown **White armies** in Siberia, the Ukraine and northwestern Russia were mounting a serious threat to Lenin's government.

In the Kremlin

After recovering from being shot, Lenin returned to his office in the **Kremlin**. He worked as hard as ever, and expected the same from others. He demanded punctuality, and sometimes fined latecomers. He forbade smoking in his presence, which annoyed many. But co-workers usually thought him considerate, and strangers meeting him for the first time were usually impressed. The British writer H.G. Wells thought that 'this amazing little man, with his frank admission of the immensity and complication of the project of Communism ... was very refreshing'.

43

Lenin expected no special privileges and took none. His wages were little more than an ordinary worker's; he ate the same food as his staff, and queued to have his hair cut like everyone else. In the winter his apartment was no better heated than any other.

Winning the war

1919 was the worst year of the **civil war**, but by its end the White armies had been repelled. Although the **peasants**, who still formed the vast majority of the population, had no great love for the Communists, they had even less for the Whites. At least the Communists had given them their land.

In 1920, the last White armies were defeated and a Polish invasion of the Ukraine was pushed back by the **Red Army** almost to the gates of Warsaw, the Polish capital. Lenin hoped the Red Army might carry **revolution** to the whole of Europe, but the Poles fought back, and by the end of the year the armies were roughly back where they had started. After three years of terrible and destructive conflict, Russia was once more at peace.

Counting the cost

The cost of the civil war was enormous. The economy was in ruins, with both industrial and agricultural production a fraction of what they had been before the revolution. The value of money had sunk and almost everything, including food, was in short supply. Life remained harsh and difficult for most Russians.

Politically, things looked better for the Communist Party – they had won the war and were in undisputed charge of the country. But victory had been achieved at a frightful cost. In order to win the war, Lenin and the senior party members (the **Politburo**) had been forced to take more and more decisions without involving the **soviets**. Power had shifted to the politburo and **democracy** in the Party was virtually dead.

Feeling the strain

Lenin was not the man he had been in 1917. He still suffered from lack of sleep, headaches and stomach problems, but, although only in his early fifties, he was now experiencing minor heart attacks. Towards the end of 1920 the death of his old love Inessa Armand, still a political colleague, hit him hard. Some friends thought he was never the same again.

Lenin knew that the revolution was nowhere near complete. It had survived the war, but if it was to survive as something worthwhile in times of peace then drastic measures needed to be taken. But which? Without the help of other revolutions in Europe there seemed no hope of a great leap forward. So perhaps, even at the moment of victory, it was time for a prudent step backwards.

◀ Lenin with Leon Trotsky (facing camera), the chief organizer of the October Revolution and founder of the Red Army. After Lenin's death he was slowly eased from power and into **exile** by Stalin and his **allies**.

10 Second thoughts?

Before Lenin could introduce the measures he thought necessary, one last titanic revolt shook his government. In March 1921, the sailors at the Kronstadt Naval Base, who had been among the most enthusiastic supporters of the revolution, rose up in rebellion, demanding a restoration of **democracy** and the powers of the **soviets**. They wanted, they said, 'a free socialist democracy.'

Lenin and his colleagues were not prepared to listen or negotiate. They thought the sailors were being dangerously unrealistic; such a policy, they thought, would risk the loss of everything that three long years of war had secured. They ordered **Red Army** units across the frozen Gulf of Finland to crush the rebellion. Thousands were killed or imprisoned.

▲ *Soldiers of the Red Army advancing across the frozen Gulf of Finland to attack the rebel-held naval fortress of Kronstadt, March 1921.*

The NEP

While the Kronstadt Naval Base was being stormed, the Communist Party was holding its Tenth Congress. It was here that Lenin formally introduced his **New Economic Policy (NEP)**. Its main features were an end to the official taking of grain from the **peasants** – from now on they were obliged to supply a fixed amount to the state but could keep or sell the rest – and the return to private ownership of businesses employing 20 workers or less. It was now legal again to trade and make a profit. There were even plans to begin trading once more with the **capitalist** countries.

This freeing-up of the economy was more popular with the country than it was with many in the party. They thought Lenin was re-introducing capitalism, and this after fighting a long war in the name of **communism**! He told them it was only a temporary retreat. To counter the dangers of loosening control over the economy, the party planned to strengthen its control over both the country and itself. The use of terror would continue, and factions or groups inside the party were banned. Anyone who refused to support agreed party policy would be expelled. The price of economic recovery was even less democracy, even less political freedom.

Illness

Getting the party to accept the NEP was hard work. By June, Lenin was so exhausted that the **Politburo** insisted he take a month off to recover in the village of Gorki, 30 kilometres (20 miles) south of Moscow. The month at Gorki turned into three months, and then six. Lenin continued to work, and often travelled into Moscow to chair meetings, but he was clearly seriously ill. The doctors brought in to examine him could not agree on what was wrong. Then, on 25 May 1922, he suffered a massive **stroke**, which paralysed his whole right side and made speaking difficult.

Krupskaya and his youngest sister Maria came to look after Lenin full time, and against most expectations he began to recover. He read books, played with a dog he had adopted, chatted with Stalin – now the Party's General Secretary and a frequent visitor – and interested himself in the nearby farm. In October 1922, he felt well enough to return to the **Kremlin** and resume some of his duties.

FOR DETAILS ON KEY PEOPLE OF LENIN'S TIME, SEE PAGES 58–9.

▲ Lenin at Gorki in August 1922, with two local children, his sister Anna (wearing hat) and his wife Nadezhda Krupskaya.

Perhaps he was fooling himself, perhaps not. He was still the most respected figure in the government; people still listened to what he had to say. Fearing that his time was short, he probably wanted to cram as much into it as possible. The future of the revolution he had led was naturally uppermost in his mind. Who should succeed him as leader and what should the policies be?

Testament

Lenin had no clear-cut favourite to succeed him, as he made clear in the letter to the Party Congress which is generally known as his 'Testament'. Trotsky, Zinoviev, Kamenev and Bukharin all had their strengths and weaknesses, according to Lenin. But he was adamant whom he did not want. Lenin had become embroiled in several disputes with Stalin over the previous year, and had also discovered that he had been very rude to Krupskaya over the telephone. Stalin, he advised the others, should be removed from his post.

Last words

'Having become general secretary, Comrade Stalin has concentrated unlimited power in his hands, and I am not sure that he will always use that power with sufficient care ... Stalin is too rude and this failing, which is entirely acceptable in relations among us Communists, is not acceptable in a general secretary. I therefore suggest that the comrades find a means of moving Stalin from this post and giving the job to someone else who is superior to Comrade Stalin in every way, that is, more patient, more loyal, more respectful and more considerate to his comrades ...'

(Excerpts from Lenin's 'Testament', written in December 1922 and January 1923)

When it came to policies Lenin's advice was less clear. He continued to believe in the necessity of terrorizing opponents of the party, but in all other respects he seemed to be becoming more moderate. In several articles written during these months, he stressed the need to reduce the size of government institutions, to learn from other countries, and to develop the revolution slowly and with caution.

How far Lenin might have gone down that road, and how much he might have rolled back the overpowering state he had done so much to create, will never be known. In March 1923, a further stroke paralysed him and took away his power of speech. This time there was no real recovery, only a sad half-life that lasted until his death on 21 January 1924. He was only 53.

A newspaper headline

'In a compartment full of fat, stodgy men, someone opened a newspaper and I saw: *Death of Lenin*. Then these men talked about the death, showing that they felt something unique and very great had passed. I looked at their faces, folk from another world, Austrian **petty-bourgeois** closed to all new ideas, lamenting the death of a **revolutionary** ...'

(Russian revolutionary Victor Serge, riding on a European train in late January 1924)

An incomplete farewell

The funeral took place six days later. Across the Union of Soviet Socialist Republics trains stopped, boats moored, factory whistles blew. In Red Square, in the heart of Moscow, the crowd sung the Communist anthem the *Internationale*, and Lenin's body was lowered into a vault in front of the Kremlin wall. The corpse did not stay there for long, however. The Politburo, allegedly at Stalin's suggestion, decided to embalm the body and lay it in a **mausoleum**. Even in death Lenin was expected to offer leadership and inspiration – to be, in effect, the immortal leader of a new religion. Krupskaya protested, but to no avail. Her wishes, like her husband's 'Testament', were ignored.

▲ *Moscow's Red Square during Lenin's funeral. The banner on the right reads, 'Lenin's grave is the cradle of liberty of humankind'.*

The second Russian revolution of 1917, the October Revolution, was probably one of the most important political events of the 20th century. Vladimir Ilyich Lenin was more responsible for bringing that revolution about than anyone else. It was he who insisted on starting the newspaper that inspired many Russian **revolutionaries**, and he who argued loudest for the sort of disciplined party which could successfully mount a revolution. From the end of his Siberian **exile** in 1900 to his seizure of power in 1917, he pushed his party to the limit, urging it to go where most members feared to tread. It was he who provided the theory, the political justification, for each daring step forward in forcefully argued pamphlets and books. Revolutions are not made by one man, but it is hard to imagine the **Bolshevik** Revolution without Lenin.

Once power had been seized, he seemed to know exactly what was required to keep it. In 1918 and in 1921, Bolshevik control was close to evaporating, but on each occasion, under great opposition, Lenin managed to force through the right measures – the Treaty of Brest-Litovsk in 1918, the **New Economic Policy (NEP)** in 1921 – to save the day. Without Lenin it is hard to believe that the Soviet Union would have lasted more than a few years.

Wider influence

Lenin's influence outside the Soviet Union was immense and continues to be significant. The changes announced and introduced by his government – like the dramatic reduction of wealth and privilege, equality for women and minority nationalities, free education and healthcare – inspired people everywhere with the promise of a better, fairer society.

Although putting these policies into practice in the Soviet Union often proved either ineffective, too costly in human suffering, or both, the fact that the country stood for such ideals was important in itself. After the Bolshevik Revolution, the Western colonial powers could never feel quite so secure again, and Lenin's political methods influenced many young revolutionaries in the poorer parts of the world, inspiring the growth of secretive, highly organized parties dedicated to the overthrow of colonial rule. For much of its existence, the Soviet Union acted as a deterrent to unrestrained **capitalism** in the poorer parts of the world and a source of support for governments at odds with the great powers of the West.

A difficult call

Inside the Soviet Union the dream of **socialism** had turned irretrievably sour within ten years of Lenin's death. By 1929, Stalin had abandoned the NEP in favour of crash industrialization and the **collectivization of agriculture**, both of which eventually brought levels of terror and intimidation – some estimates claim 20 million deaths – undreamt of in Lenin's day. How responsible was Lenin for the mistakes and evils of his successors? Was the Soviet Union he left behind inevitably doomed to this sort of fate?

▶ *Five days after Lenin's death, General Secretary Stalin promises the Communist Party of the Soviet Union that he will continue Lenin's work.*

These are difficult questions to answer. There are two clear arguments in Lenin's favour. First, he did try to get rid of Stalin, and could hardly be held responsible for the other Bolshevik leaders' failure to take notice of his 'Testament'. Secondly, he argued for a slow pace of development and a lessening of state control in the last months of his active political life. He had an all too brief period in which to address the problems that faced Russia at the end of the **civil war**, before the onset of his illness. If Lenin had lived longer, some say that the Soviet Union might have revealed a more human face to the rest of the world.

There are two strong arguments against this. Firstly, it was Lenin, after all, who founded the **Cheka**, and encouraged its use of terror as a political weapon. Perhaps the survival of the regime during the civil war necessitated harsh methods, but the NEP was then used to justify more of the same after the war. Lenin found it all too easy to repress his own compassion when reason told him that others' suffering was necessary for the good of the revolution. He does not seem to have asked himself whether a revolution that needed to defend itself in this way for the foreseeable future was worth having.

Mind over feelings

'Often I can't listen to music. It acts on my nerves. It makes one want to say a lot of sweet nonsense and stroke the heads of people who live in a filthy hell-hole and yet can create such beauty. But you can't stroke anyone's head today – you'll get your hands cut off. The need is to beat them over the head, beat them mercilessly even though we, as an ideal, are against any coercion of [violence against] people. Hm, hm … it's a hellishly difficult necessity.'

(Lenin in conversation with the Russian writer Maxim Gorky, explaining what he sees as the sad necessity of revolutionary violence)

Secondly, Lenin closed down **democracy** in the country at large, and then inside his own party as well. He always had good arguments for this, but the suspicion remains that the only person he trusted to be in charge was himself. Lenin had no intellectual humility. He always thought he knew best, and tended to distrust the motives of anyone who disagreed with him. He was **undemocratic** by nature.

An inspiration and a warning

In the Soviet Union, Lenin remained a national hero right up until the fall of **communism**; his face stared down from schoolroom walls, his statues adorned city squares. Each day thousands of Soviet citizens and foreign tourists visited his embalmed body in its Red Square **mausoleum**.

Now that Russia and the rest of the former Soviet Union have abandoned communism, he has become less of a living symbol and more of an historical figure. The ideals which inspired the Bolshevik Revolution, and which, in the end, were so completely betrayed by it, are still alive in the world today. Lenin, who played a huge part in making that revolution and had at least some part in the betrayal of its promise, now serves as both an inspiration and a warning to those who seek to follow in his footsteps.

▼ *A queue of visitors to Lenin's mausoleum.*

Timeline

1870	Vladimir Ilyich Ulyanov (later called Lenin) is born on 10 April in Simbirsk.
1879	Vladimir begins schooling at the Simbirsk Gimnazia.
1886	His father dies.
1887	His older brother Alexander is executed for planning to assassinate the **Tsar**. Vladimir finishes his schooling and enrols at Kazan University. In December he is expelled for taking part in student protests.
1890–91	Ulyanov takes a law degree as an **external student** at **St Petersburg** University, and works as a barrister in Samara.
1893	Moves to St Petersburg.
1895	Visits leading Russian **Marxists** in western and central Europe. Arrested in St Petersburg for illegal political activities.
1895–97	In prison in St Petersburg.
1897	**Exiled** to Siberia.
1898	Marries Nadezhda Krupskaya. Russian Social-Democratic Labour Party formed.
1900	Lenin released from Siberian exile. Travels to Western Europe. *Iskra* published.
1901	Lenin writes *What is to be Done?*
1903	Russian Social-Democratic Labour Party splits into **Bolshevik** and **Menshevik** factions.
1905	A year of political turmoil in Russia. Lenin returns to Russia in November.
1906	Moves to Finland to avoid arrest.
1907	Returns to western Europe.
1908–12	Lives in Paris.
1912–14	Lives in Galicia, a Polish area of the Austro-Hungarian Empire.
1914	World War I begins.

1914–17	Lenin lives in Switzerland. Writes *Imperialism: The Highest Stage of Capitalism*.
1917	February: First Russian Revolution takes place.
	April: Lenin arrives back in Russia, and produces his 'April Theses'.
	July: Forced into hiding.
	October: Second Russian Revolution brings the Bolsheviks to power.
	Decrees on an end to the war and giving land to the **peasants**.
	Establishment of the **Cheka**.
1918	The closing down of the Constituent Assembly.
	The signing of the Treaty of Brest-Litovsk.
	The execution of the Tsar and his family.
1918–20	**Civil war** in Russia.
1921	Kronstadt Rebellion.
	Introduction of the **New Economic Policy (NEP)**.
	Lenin's health deteriorates.
1922	He suffers a massive **stroke** in May.
1922–23	In December–February, he writes Letter to Congress (his 'Testament'), which is critical of Stalin, and several articles recommending a moderation of the revolution.
	Suffers another massive stroke in March 1923.
1924	Lenin dies on 21 January at the age of 53. His body is embalmed and placed in a **mausoleum** in Red Square.
1929	After several years of fighting between Russian groups, Stalin emerges as the single leader of the Soviet Union and enforces a third revolution, featuring a crash industrialization programme, overall state planning and the **collectivization of agriculture**.
1989–91	Collapse of **communism** and the disintegration of the Soviet Union into fifteen separate states.

Key people of Lenin's time

Bukharin, Nikolai Ivanovich (1888–1938). Born in Moscow, Bukharin became politically active as a student during the 1905 revolution. He lived as a **revolutionary** inside Russia until 1912, when he was arrested and **exiled**. He escaped to western Europe and returned to Russia in 1917. While there was a chance of further revolutions in Europe he argued for the **Bolsheviks** to make trouble wherever they could, but when it became clear that these revolutions would not take place he joined Lenin in arguing for a slow and peaceful progress towards **socialism** in Russia. He was executed by Stalin in 1938.

Gorky, Maxim (1868–1936). Russian writer who was also involved in revolutionary politics. Briefly imprisoned in 1905 and then lived in western European exile until 1917. He became both a supporter of the Bolshevik Revolution and an important critic of its excesses.

Kamenev, Lev Borisovich (1883–1936). A revolutionary from 1901 and a leading Bolshevik in the period leading up to the seizure of power in 1917, which, along with Zinoviev, he initially opposed. After the revolution he was in charge of the Moscow **Communist** Party organization. He was executed by Stalin in 1936.

Martov, Yuli Osipovich (1873–1923). Russian **Marxist** and one of Lenin's closest colleagues in his early St Petersburg days. They fell out in 1903, and Martov became one of the leading **Mensheviks**. He opposed the Bolsheviks after 1917, went into voluntary exile in 1921, and died in Berlin two years later.

Marx, Karl (1818–83). German **philosopher**, economist and political scientist whose theories of social development helped to inspire both socialism and communism (see box on page 13).

Plekhanov, Georgi Valentinovich (1857–1918). Seen as the founder of Russian **Marxism**. He founded the Emancipation of Labour Group in 1883 and helped to found the Russian Social-Democratic Labour Party in 1898. He fell out with Lenin in 1903, partly on political, partly on personal grounds, and joined the Mensheviks. He was not an active figure in the revolutions of 1917.

Stalin, Joseph Vissarionovich (1878–1953). Born Joseph Djugashvili in Georgia. An active member of the Russian Social-Democratic Labour Party from around 1900 and a Bolshevik from 1903. He endured many periods of Siberian exile between then and the revolution. In 1917, he was appointed **Commissar** for Nationalities, and in 1922 he was appointed to the powerful position of General Secretary of the Communist Party. He survived the criticism included in Lenin's 'Testament', out-manoeuvred his opponents in the party, and established a one-man **dictatorship** over the Soviet Union. He introduced the programme of crash industrialization (the five year plans), **collectivization of agriculture**, and instituted a reign of terror over the Soviet population which saw many millions either killed or sent to gulags (prison labour camps).

Trotsky, Leon (1879–1940). Born Lev Davidovich Bronstein in Yanovka, Ukraine. As a young Jewish revolutionary, he was arrested and exiled to Siberia in 1898. He escaped to Western Europe in 1902, but returned to play a starring role as leader of the St Petersburg **Soviet** of Workers' Deputies in the 1905 Russian revolution. A great speaker and writer, he worked as a journalist in the West until 1917, when he returned again to Russia. He joined the Bolsheviks, supported Lenin when he argued for a Bolshevik revolution, and played a major role in organizing the seizure of power. As Lenin's Commissar of War, he created the **Red Army** and led it to victory in the Russian **Civil War**. After Lenin's death jealous colleagues and the single-minded Stalin eased him from power. In 1940, he was murdered in Mexico by one of Stalin's secret agents.

Ulyanov, Alexander Ilyich (1866–87). Lenin's older brother, who was executed by the regime of **Tsar** Alexander III for his part in planning an attempt on the Tsar's life.

Zinoviev, Grigori (1883–1936) A revolutionary from around 1900 and a leading Bolshevik in the period leading up to the seizure of power in 1917, which, along with Kamenev, he initially opposed. After the revolution he was in charge of the Petrograd (later Leningrad) Party organization. An inspiring speaker, he was head of the Communist International from 1919 to 1926. He was executed by Stalin in 1936.

Further reading & other resources

Further reading

Joseph Stalin (Leading Lives series), David Downing, Heinemann Library, 2001

Key Battles of World War I (20th Century Perspectives series), David Taylor, Heinemann Library, 2001

Russia and the USSR 1905–56 (History Through Sources series), Nigel Kelly, Heinemann, 1998

Sources

Lenin, Robert Service, Macmillan, 2000

Memoirs of a Revolutionary, Victor Serge, Oxford University Press, 1963

Ten Days that Shook the World, John Reed, Penguin, 1966

Three Who Made a Revolution, Bertram Wolfe, Pelican, 1966

Films

Battleship Potemkin (directed by Sergei Eisenstein, 1925)

Dr Zhivago (based on the novel by Boris Pasternak, starring Julie Christie and Omar Sharif, directed by David Lean, 1965)

Reds (starring Warren Beatty and Diane Keaton, directed by Warren Beatty, 1981)

Websites

Lenin Internet Archive:
    www.marxists.org/archive/lenin

Time 100: Leaders and Revolutionaries – V. I. Lenin:
    www.time.com/time/time100/leaders/profile/lenin.html

The Columbia Electronic Encyclopedia:
    www.encyclopedia.com/articles/07362.html

The publishers would like to thank the following for permission to reproduce copyright material: Chrysalis Books Ltd: pp. 30, 34, 43; Oxford University Press for material from *The Cheka: Lenin's Political Force* by George Leggett (1981): p.49.

Glossary

allies people or countries that believe in and/or fight for the same things

armed insurrection violent uprising against the government

Bolsheviks one of the two political parties that emerged from the 1903 split in the Russian Social-Democratic Labour Party. *Bolshevik* is Russian for 'those with a majority' (the Mensheviks were the other party).

bourgeoisie the capitalist class – those who own the industries and banks

capitalism economic system in which the production and distribution of goods depend on private wealth and profit-making

Cheka the Extraordinary Commission for Combating Counter-Revolution and Sabotage: the political police force created by Lenin in December 1917. After World War II it was called the KGB.

civil rights legal rights of all people to the same equal opportunities and benefits

civil war war between different groups within one country

collectivization of agriculture creation of large, jointly owned farms by joining together small farms which had previously been privately owned

Comintern the Communist International, an organization formed by the world's communist parties worldwide with the aim of promoting world revolution

(People's) Commissar position of authority in Sovnarkom (the Bolshevik government after October 1917) with particular responsibility for one area of government. Stalin, for example, was Commissar for Nationalities.

communism according to Karl Marx, the stage of history that would follow socialism. In this stage, free people would share with each other in a situation of economic plenty. The name was adopted by the Bolsheviks and became associated with the system of economic planning and political dictatorship developed in the Soviet Union in the mid-20th century under Lenin, Stalin and their successors.

democracy political system in which governments are regularly elected by the mass of the people, or country in which this system exists

dictatorship government by an individual (called a dictator) or a small group that does not allow the mass of the people any say in how they are governed

exile the punishment of being sent away. In Tsarist Russia, exile to remote and inhospitable parts of the country like Siberia was a common punishment.

external student person who studies from home rather than attending a college

Kremlin walled fortress in Moscow that has been the traditional home of Russian leaders almost continuously since the 12th century

Marxism the ideas of Karl Marx; a person who believes and acts according to these ideas is a **Marxist**

mausoleum large tomb or resting place for the dead

Mensheviks one of the two political parties that emerged from the 1903 split in the Russian Social-Democratic Labour Party. *Menshevik* is Russian for 'those in a minority' (the Bolsheviks were the other party).

monarchy government ruled by a king, queen, emperor, empress, tsar or tsarina

New Economic Policy (NEP) the re-introduction of limited or private trading which followed the Russian Civil War

peasant farmer or farm worker with little or no farm land of their own

petty-bourgeois lower middle class

philosopher person who thinks about, analyses and describes the causes and nature of life and human existence

Politburo Soviet government cabinet (or small ruling committee)

Red Army originally the army formed by the Bolsheviks to defend their revolution in the civil war. After the civil war it became the official army of the Soviet Union.

revolution in politics, working to overthrow the existing order in its entirety – not being content with merely swapping one group of individuals for another

St Petersburg city on the Gulf of Finland, capital of the Russian Empire. Renamed Petrograd in 1914, Leningrad in 1924, its name reverted to St Petersburg once more in 1991.

socialism way of organizing society that puts the needs of the community above the short-term wants or needs of the individual; a person who believes in this type of government is a **socialist**

soviet Russian for 'council'

Sovnarkom abbreviation of the Russian term for the Council of People's Commissars, the Bolshevik government formed in 1917

stroke a disabling interruption in the flow of blood to the brain

terrorist someone who uses violence to achieve political ends

trade unions organizations formed to protect and advance the pay and conditions of workers

tsar (or czar) hereditary ruler of the Russian Empire, similar to king or emperor; a woman was a tsarina

undemocratic not taking account of the wishes of the people

White armies armies fighting against the 'red' Bolsheviks in the civil war. Some White armies wanted to bring back the tsar; others to restore the government which existed between the two revolutions in 1917.

women's rights the rights of women to legal and social equality with men

Index